Copyright © 2023 by Cameron Bailey (Author)
All rights reserved. No part of this book may be reproduced or utilized in any form or by any means, electronic or mechanical, including photocopying, recording or by any information storage and retrieval system, without permission in writing from the publisher, except for brief quotations in critical articles or reviews.

The content of this book is based on various sources and is intended for educational and entertainment purposes only. While the author has made every effort to ensure the accuracy, completeness, and reliability of the information provided, the information may be subject to errors, omissions, or inaccuracies. Therefore, the author makes no warranties, express or implied, regarding the content of this book.

Readers are advised to seek the guidance of a licensed professional before attempting any techniques or actions outlined in this book. The author is not responsible for any losses, damages, or injuries that may arise from the use of information contained within. The information provided in this book is not intended to be a substitute for professional advice, and readers should not rely solely on the information presented.

By reading this book, readers acknowledge that the author is not providing legal, financial, medical, or professional advice. Any reliance on the information contained in this book is solely at the reader's own risk.

Thank you for selecting this book as a valuable source of knowledge and inspiration. Our aim is to provide you with insights and information that will enrich your understanding and enhance your personal growth. We appreciate your decision to embark on this journey of discovery with us, and we hope that this book will exceed your expectations and leave a lasting impact on your life.

Title: Maintaining Your Confidence
Subtitle: Strategies for Sustaining a Positive Mindset and Overcoming Obstacles

Series: The Secrets of Self-Confidence: A Comprehensive Guide to Achieving Your Goals
Author: Cameron Bailey

Table of Contents

Introduction 5
What is self-confidence? 5
Why is it important to maintain your self-confidence? 8
How to maintain your self-confidence 11

Chapter 1: The importance of maintaining your self-confidence 14
Self-confidence is essential for a happy and successful life 14
When you have self-confidence, you are more likely to take risks, achieve your goals, and be happy with your life 16
There are many things you can do to maintain your self-confidence 18

Chapter 2: How to maintain your self-confidence . 21
Identify your self-confidence blocks 21
Challenge your negative thoughts 23
Focus on your strengths 25
Set realistic goals 27
Take risks 29
Surround yourself with positive people 31
Practice positive self-talk 34

Chapter 3: Dealing with setbacks 37
Don't give up 37

Learn from your mistakes *40*
Don't compare yourself to others *43*
Celebrate your successes *46*

Chapter 4: Finding your inner confidence **50**
What is inner confidence? *50*
How to find your inner confidence *54*

Chapter 5: Rebuilding your self-confidence after a setback **58**
It's okay to feel down after a setback *58*
Don't beat yourself up *60*
Focus on the positive *63*
Seek help if you need it *66*

Conclusion **71**
The importance of inner confidence *71*
How to continue to build your inner confidence *74*

Wordbook **77**
Supplementary Materials **79**

Introduction
What is self-confidence?

Self-confidence is a crucial aspect of an individual's personality. It is the belief in one's abilities, qualities, and judgment, which leads to the individual's self-assurance and positive outlook on life. Self-confidence helps individuals feel better about themselves, take risks, make decisions, and handle challenges more effectively. It is an essential ingredient for a happy and successful life.

What is self-confidence?

Self-confidence is the belief in oneself and one's abilities. It is the assurance that one can accomplish what one sets out to do. Self-confidence involves a sense of self-assurance and a belief in one's value and worth as a person. It is not an inherent trait; rather, it is something that can be developed and nurtured.

Self-confidence is built on a foundation of self-esteem. Self-esteem is the opinion an individual has of themselves, which is influenced by their experiences, upbringing, and interactions with others. A person with high self-esteem values themselves and believes they are worthy of respect, love, and attention. On the other hand, a person with low self-esteem struggles to value themselves and may feel inferior or inadequate compared to others.

Self-confidence can also be affected by external factors, such as the environment, culture, and societal expectations. For example, a person raised in an environment where they were consistently praised and supported is likely to have higher self-confidence than someone who grew up in a critical and unsupportive environment. Similarly, societal expectations and cultural norms can impact a person's self-confidence, as they may feel pressure to conform to certain standards and expectations.

The benefits of self-confidence are numerous. It allows individuals to take risks and pursue their goals without fear of failure. It helps individuals to trust their own judgment and make decisions with conviction. Self-confident individuals are generally more resilient and better equipped to handle setbacks and challenges. They are also more likely to be successful in their personal and professional lives.

However, self-confidence can also be a double-edged sword. Overconfidence can lead to complacency and a lack of self-awareness, which can ultimately lead to failure. It is crucial to strike a balance between self-confidence and self-awareness.

In conclusion, self-confidence is the belief in oneself and one's abilities. It is built on a foundation of self-esteem and can be influenced by external factors such as the environment and societal expectations. Self-confidence is essential for a happy and successful life, but it is important to strike a balance between self-confidence and self-awareness.

Why is it important to maintain your self-confidence?

Self-confidence is a critical aspect of an individual's well-being, and it plays a significant role in determining one's success in life. It is the foundation upon which individuals build their lives and their relationships. Without self-confidence, individuals may struggle to achieve their goals and may find it difficult to navigate the challenges and uncertainties of life. Maintaining self-confidence is, therefore, essential to living a happy and fulfilling life.

Why is it important to maintain your self-confidence?

1. Self-confidence allows you to pursue your goals:

Maintaining self-confidence is crucial if you want to pursue your goals in life. Self-confidence helps you to believe in yourself and your abilities, giving you the motivation and courage to take action towards achieving your goals. Without self-confidence, you may doubt your abilities and shy away from taking action, ultimately preventing you from reaching your full potential.

2. Self-confidence helps you deal with challenges:

Life is full of challenges, and maintaining self-confidence is crucial to dealing with them effectively. Self-confident individuals are better equipped to handle setbacks and challenges as they believe in themselves and their ability to overcome obstacles. They are also more resilient and are better able to bounce back from setbacks and failures.

3. Self-confidence improves your relationships:

Maintaining self-confidence is also essential for building and maintaining healthy relationships. Self-confident individuals are better able to communicate effectively, assert their needs, and set healthy boundaries. They are also less likely to be intimidated by others, allowing them to build stronger and more fulfilling relationships.

4. Self-confidence improves your mental and emotional well-being:

Maintaining self-confidence is crucial for good mental and emotional health. Self-confidence helps individuals to feel good about themselves, promoting a positive self-image and reducing feelings of anxiety and depression. It also helps individuals to manage stress more effectively, improving their overall quality of life.

5. Self-confidence is essential for career success:

Finally, maintaining self-confidence is critical to career success. Self-confident individuals are more likely to take risks, speak up for themselves, and pursue career opportunities that align with their goals and aspirations. They are also more likely to be successful in their careers, as they believe in themselves and their abilities.

In conclusion, maintaining self-confidence is essential for living a happy and fulfilling life. Self-confidence allows individuals to pursue their goals, deal with challenges, improve their relationships, promote good mental and emotional well-being, and achieve career success. It is, therefore, important to invest in building and maintaining self-confidence throughout your life.

How to maintain your self-confidence

Maintaining self-confidence is crucial to achieving success in life. It allows individuals to pursue their goals, deal with challenges, improve their relationships, promote good mental and emotional well-being, and achieve career success. However, maintaining self-confidence can be a challenge, especially in the face of setbacks and obstacles. In this chapter, we will explore some effective strategies for maintaining self-confidence.

How to maintain your self-confidence

1. Identify your self-confidence blocks:

The first step in maintaining self-confidence is to identify the factors that are blocking it. Self-confidence blocks can be internal, such as negative self-talk, self-doubt, and fear of failure, or external, such as criticism from others, unrealistic expectations, and social pressure. Once you identify your self-confidence blocks, you can take steps to address them.

2. Challenge your negative thoughts:

Negative thoughts are a common self-confidence block. They can hold you back, make you doubt yourself, and prevent you from taking action. To maintain self-confidence, it's essential to challenge your negative thoughts and replace them with positive, affirming thoughts. For example, instead of thinking, "I can't do this," replace it with "I can do this."

3. Focus on your strengths:

Focusing on your strengths is an effective way to maintain self-confidence. By acknowledging your strengths and abilities, you can boost your self-esteem and believe in yourself. Make a list of your strengths and achievements and refer to it regularly to remind yourself of your capabilities.

4. Set realistic goals:

Setting realistic goals is crucial to maintaining self-confidence. Unrealistic goals can be overwhelming and may set you up for failure, leading to a loss of self-confidence. On the other hand, setting achievable goals can give you a sense of accomplishment, boost your self-esteem, and help you maintain your self-confidence.

5. Take risks:

Taking risks is an essential part of maintaining self-confidence. When you take risks, you step out of your comfort zone and challenge yourself. This can lead to personal growth and a sense of accomplishment, which can boost your self-confidence. Remember, taking risks doesn't mean being reckless, but rather taking calculated risks that align with your goals and aspirations.

6. Surround yourself with positive people:

Surrounding yourself with positive, supportive people is essential to maintaining self-confidence. Positive people can lift you up, encourage you, and believe in you, which can boost your self-esteem and help you maintain your self-confidence. On the other hand, negative people can bring you down, make you doubt yourself, and drain your energy, which can hurt your self-confidence.

7. Practice positive self-talk:

Positive self-talk is an effective way to maintain self-confidence. It involves using positive, affirming statements to boost your self-esteem and promote a positive self-image. For example, instead of saying, "I'm not good enough," say, "I am capable and competent." Practice positive self-talk regularly, and it will become a habit.

Conclusion:

Maintaining self-confidence is crucial to achieving success and living a happy and fulfilling life. By identifying your self-confidence blocks, challenging your negative thoughts, focusing on your strengths, setting realistic goals, taking risks, surrounding yourself with positive people, and practicing positive self-talk, you can maintain your self-confidence and achieve your goals. Remember, self-confidence is a journey, and it requires effort and commitment, but it is worth it in the end.

Chapter 1: The importance of maintaining your self-confidence

Self-confidence is essential for a happy and successful life

Self-confidence is an essential ingredient for a happy and successful life. It's the belief in oneself that helps you tackle challenges, overcome obstacles, and achieve your goals. Without self-confidence, you may feel inadequate, powerless, and unable to pursue your dreams. In this chapter, we'll explore why self-confidence is crucial for your well-being and how it can impact your life.

Firstly, self-confidence is essential for your mental health. When you have confidence in yourself, you're less likely to experience anxiety, depression, and other mental health problems. You're also better equipped to handle stress and manage difficult emotions. A lack of self-confidence, on the other hand, can lead to negative self-talk, self-doubt, and a constant feeling of inadequacy, which can have detrimental effects on your mental health.

Secondly, self-confidence is crucial for your relationships. When you have confidence in yourself, you're more likely to form healthy, positive relationships. You're able to set boundaries, communicate your needs, and assert yourself in a respectful and confident manner. A lack of self-confidence can lead to people-pleasing, codependency, and unhealthy relationships, where you may find yourself sacrificing your own needs and desires for the sake of others.

Thirdly, self-confidence is essential for your career. When you have confidence in yourself, you're more likely to take risks, speak up, and pursue new opportunities. You're able to handle rejection and setbacks without giving up, and you're more likely to succeed in your professional life. A lack of self-confidence, on the other hand, can hold you back from reaching your full potential and achieving your career goals.

In summary, self-confidence is essential for a happy and successful life. It's the belief in oneself that helps you tackle challenges, overcome obstacles, and achieve your goals. It's crucial for your mental health, relationships, and career. Without self-confidence, you may feel inadequate, powerless, and unable to pursue your dreams.

When you have self-confidence, you are more likely to take risks, achieve your goals, and be happy with your life

When you have self-confidence, you are more likely to take risks, achieve your goals, and be happy with your life. In this chapter, we'll explore why self-confidence is crucial for taking risks, achieving goals, and experiencing happiness, and how to cultivate it in your life.

Firstly, self-confidence is essential for taking risks. When you have confidence in yourself, you're more likely to step outside of your comfort zone and take on new challenges. You're less afraid of failure and more focused on the potential rewards of your actions. This mindset can lead to new opportunities and experiences that you may have otherwise missed out on.

Secondly, self-confidence is crucial for achieving goals. When you have confidence in yourself, you're more likely to set challenging but achievable goals, and work towards them with determination and persistence. You believe in your ability to succeed, which can help you overcome obstacles and setbacks along the way. This can lead to a sense of accomplishment and fulfillment when you achieve your goals.

Thirdly, self-confidence is essential for experiencing happiness. When you have confidence in yourself, you're more likely to feel positive about your life and your abilities. This can lead to a greater sense of satisfaction and happiness with yourself and your life. You're also more likely to seek out and engage in activities that bring you joy and fulfillment.

So how can you cultivate self-confidence in your life? One way is to focus on your strengths and accomplishments. Recognize your skills and abilities, and take pride in your achievements. Another way is to challenge your negative self-talk and replace it with positive affirmations. Practice self-compassion and remind yourself that everyone makes mistakes and experiences setbacks. Finally, surround yourself with positive and supportive people who believe in you and your abilities.

In summary, self-confidence is crucial for taking risks, achieving goals, and experiencing happiness. It's essential for stepping outside of your comfort zone, pursuing your dreams, and feeling positive about your life. You can cultivate self-confidence by focusing on your strengths and accomplishments, challenging your negative self-talk, and surrounding yourself with positive and supportive people.

There are many things you can do to maintain your self-confidence

There are many things you can do to maintain your self-confidence. In this chapter, we'll explore some of the key strategies and techniques you can use to boost and sustain your confidence over time.

1. Identify and challenge negative thoughts

Negative thoughts and self-doubt can erode your confidence over time. It's essential to identify and challenge these thoughts when they arise. One way to do this is to practice mindfulness and observe your thoughts without judgment. When negative thoughts arise, question their validity and replace them with positive affirmations.

2. Set achievable goals

Setting achievable goals can help build confidence and motivation. Start by setting small, realistic goals, and gradually work your way up to more significant challenges. Celebrate your successes along the way, and learn from any setbacks or failures.

3. Focus on your strengths

Focusing on your strengths can help you recognize your worth and value. Make a list of your skills and abilities, and remind yourself of them regularly. Consider how you can use your strengths to achieve your goals and overcome challenges.

4. Take care of your physical and mental health

Taking care of your physical and mental health is crucial for maintaining confidence. Exercise regularly, eat a balanced and healthy diet, and get enough sleep. Practice stress-reducing techniques such as meditation or yoga, and seek support from a mental health professional if needed.

5. Surround yourself with positive and supportive people

Surrounding yourself with positive and supportive people can help boost your confidence and provide encouragement when you need it. Seek out friends, family, or colleagues who believe in you and your abilities. Avoid people who bring you down or undermine your confidence.

6. Practice self-compassion

Practice self-compassion and treat yourself with kindness and understanding. Remember that everyone makes mistakes and experiences setbacks. Treat yourself as you would treat a good friend who is struggling.

7. Continuously learn and grow

Continuously learning and growing can help you build confidence and self-esteem. Take classes or workshops to develop new skills, read books on self-improvement or personal growth, and seek out new experiences that challenge you.

In summary, maintaining self-confidence requires ongoing effort and commitment. By identifying and challenging negative thoughts, setting achievable goals, focusing on your strengths, taking care of your physical and mental health, surrounding yourself with positive and supportive people, practicing self-compassion, and continuously learning and growing, you can cultivate and maintain self-confidence over time.

Chapter 2: How to maintain your self-confidence
Identify your self-confidence blocks

Identifying your self-confidence blocks is an important step in maintaining your self-confidence. These blocks can come from internal or external sources and can prevent you from achieving your goals or feeling good about yourself. Here are some strategies for identifying and overcoming self-confidence blocks:

1. Reflect on your past experiences: Think about times when you felt confident and times when you didn't. What was different about those situations? What beliefs or thoughts were present in each situation? Identifying these patterns can help you understand your self-confidence blocks.

2. Notice your negative self-talk: Pay attention to your inner dialogue. Are you constantly criticizing yourself? Do you tell yourself you're not good enough? These negative thoughts can erode your self-confidence over time.

3. Identify limiting beliefs: Limiting beliefs are thoughts or beliefs that hold you back from achieving your goals. Examples of limiting beliefs include "I'm not smart enough," "I'm not good at public speaking," or "I'll never be successful." Identify your limiting beliefs and challenge them.

4. Consider your environment: Your environment can have a big impact on your self-confidence. Are you surrounded by supportive people who lift you up? Or are you surrounded by negative people who bring you down? Take a look at the people and situations in your life and assess whether they are contributing to or detracting from your self-confidence.

5. Seek feedback: Ask trusted friends, family members, or colleagues for feedback on your strengths and areas for improvement. This can help you gain a better understanding of your abilities and build your self-confidence.

6. Practice self-compassion: Remember to be kind to yourself. Everyone makes mistakes and experiences setbacks. Don't beat yourself up when things don't go as planned. Practice self-compassion and treat yourself with the same kindness and understanding you would offer a good friend.

By identifying your self-confidence blocks, you can take steps to overcome them and maintain a healthy level of self-confidence. Remember that building self-confidence is a process and requires ongoing effort and self-reflection.

Challenge your negative thoughts

Negative thoughts can be harmful to your self-confidence and your overall well-being. They can make you doubt yourself, feel anxious or depressed, and hold you back from achieving your goals. It's important to challenge these negative thoughts so that you can replace them with more positive and empowering ones. Here are some strategies that can help you challenge your negative thoughts:

1. Identify your negative thoughts: Start by paying attention to your thoughts and identifying when they turn negative. Write down these negative thoughts in a journal or on a piece of paper.

2. Question the evidence: Once you have identified your negative thoughts, challenge the evidence behind them. Ask yourself if there is any evidence to support these thoughts. If not, then they may be irrational or unfounded.

3. Consider alternative explanations: Try to come up with alternative explanations for the situation that is causing your negative thoughts. Think about other factors that may be contributing to the situation and consider how you might approach it differently.

4. Look for evidence to the contrary: Look for evidence that contradicts your negative thoughts. For example, if you're feeling like a failure because you didn't get

a job offer, remind yourself of all the times you have succeeded in the past.

5. Practice positive self-talk: Replace your negative thoughts with positive affirmations. For example, if you catch yourself thinking "I'm never going to be able to do this," replace it with "I can do this if I put in the effort."

6. Use cognitive restructuring: This technique involves replacing your negative thoughts with positive ones by actively challenging and changing the way you think about a situation. For example, instead of thinking "I'm never going to be good enough," reframe it as "I may have some weaknesses, but I also have strengths that I can build on."

7. Practice mindfulness: Mindfulness can help you become more aware of your thoughts and emotions. This can help you identify negative thoughts and challenge them in the moment.

Challenging your negative thoughts can be difficult at first, but with practice, it can become easier. Remember to be patient with yourself and celebrate small successes along the way. By replacing negative thoughts with more positive and empowering ones, you can improve your self-confidence and achieve your goals.

Focus on your strengths

Focusing on your strengths is a key aspect of maintaining self-confidence. When you focus on what you're good at and what you enjoy doing, you can build a sense of accomplishment and purpose that can help sustain your confidence over time. Here are some tips for focusing on your strengths:

1. Identify your strengths: Take some time to reflect on what you're good at. Think about activities that come naturally to you, and those that you enjoy doing. Consider skills that you've developed over time, and those that have been recognized by others.

2. Use your strengths: Once you've identified your strengths, find ways to use them in your daily life. Look for opportunities at work or in your personal life where you can apply your skills and expertise. When you're using your strengths, you're likely to feel more engaged and motivated, which can boost your self-confidence.

3. Set goals that leverage your strengths: When setting goals for yourself, think about how you can use your strengths to achieve them. For example, if you're good at public speaking, you might set a goal to give a presentation at work or to speak at a community event. By setting goals

that leverage your strengths, you'll be more likely to achieve them and feel good about your accomplishments.

4. Celebrate your successes: When you achieve something that leverages your strengths, take time to celebrate your success. This can help build a positive association between your strengths and your sense of accomplishment, which can further boost your self-confidence.

5. Surround yourself with supportive people: When you're trying to focus on your strengths, it's important to surround yourself with people who support and encourage you. Seek out friends, family members, or colleagues who appreciate your strengths and can help you build on them. When you're around supportive people, you're more likely to feel confident and capable.

Set realistic goals

Setting realistic goals is an important aspect of maintaining self-confidence. When you set goals that are achievable, you set yourself up for success, which in turn helps to build and maintain your confidence. Here are some tips on setting realistic goals:

1. Identify your values: Before setting goals, it's important to identify what is most important to you. What do you value in life? What are your priorities? Once you have a clear understanding of your values, you can set goals that align with them.

2. Make them specific: Specific goals are easier to achieve than vague goals. When setting goals, make them as specific as possible. For example, instead of setting a goal to "lose weight," set a goal to "lose 10 pounds in the next three months."

3. Make them measurable: Measurable goals are also easier to achieve. When you can measure your progress, you'll know when you've achieved your goal. For example, if your goal is to run a 5K, you can measure your progress by tracking your running times.

4. Make them achievable: Setting goals that are too difficult or impossible to achieve can be demotivating. Make

sure your goals are achievable with the resources you have available.

5. Make them relevant: Goals that are relevant to your life and values are more likely to be achieved. Make sure your goals align with what you want to achieve in life.

6. Make them time-bound: Setting a deadline for your goals can help to keep you motivated and on track. Make sure your goals have a specific time frame for completion.

7. Break them down: Sometimes, big goals can seem overwhelming. To make them more manageable, break them down into smaller, more achievable goals. This will help you to stay motivated and make progress towards your ultimate goal.

By setting realistic goals, you'll be able to build and maintain your self-confidence. Remember to celebrate your achievements along the way, and don't be afraid to adjust your goals as needed. With practice, you'll become better at setting realistic goals and achieving them.

Take risks

Taking risks is an important part of maintaining self-confidence. It involves stepping out of your comfort zone and challenging yourself to try new things. When you take risks, you can grow and learn from new experiences, which can lead to increased self-confidence. However, taking risks can also be scary and intimidating, and it can be difficult to know where to start. Here are some strategies for taking risks and building your self-confidence:

1. Start small: Taking small risks can help build your confidence and prepare you for bigger challenges. For example, you might try a new type of food or take a different route to work. Celebrate these small victories to build momentum.

2. Break down bigger goals into smaller steps: If you have a bigger goal that feels overwhelming, break it down into smaller, achievable steps. This will help you see progress along the way and build confidence as you go.

3. Embrace failure: Taking risks involves the possibility of failure, but this doesn't mean that failure is a bad thing. Embrace failure as an opportunity to learn and grow, rather than a sign of defeat. Remember that everyone fails at some point, and it's often the people who keep trying who ultimately succeed.

4. Visualize success: Before taking a risk, take some time to visualize yourself succeeding. This can help build confidence and prepare you mentally for the challenge ahead.

5. Use positive self-talk: Encourage yourself with positive self-talk before and during a risky situation. Remind yourself of your strengths and past successes to build confidence and help you stay focused.

6. Surround yourself with supportive people: Having a support system can be invaluable when taking risks. Surround yourself with people who believe in you and encourage you to take chances. This can help you build confidence and feel more prepared to take on challenges.

7. Keep learning: Continuous learning and personal growth can help build self-confidence over time. By learning new skills and trying new things, you can gain confidence in your abilities and feel more prepared to take risks in the future.

Remember, taking risks is not about being reckless or impulsive. It's about stepping outside of your comfort zone and challenging yourself to grow and learn. By taking calculated risks and using these strategies to build your self-confidence, you can achieve greater success and fulfillment in life.

Surround yourself with positive people

The people you surround yourself with have a significant impact on your self-confidence. Positive people can help boost your self-esteem, while negative people can bring you down and sap your self-confidence. If you want to maintain your self-confidence, it's important to surround yourself with positive people. In this section, we'll explore why this is so important and offer some tips for finding and surrounding yourself with positive people.

Why Positive People are Important

When you spend time with positive people, you'll likely experience several benefits that can help boost your self-confidence:

1. Positive people can provide support: Positive people are often supportive of others and can offer you the emotional support you need to maintain your self-confidence. They can provide you with encouragement, advice, and a listening ear when you need it.

2. Positive people can help you see things differently: Negative people tend to focus on problems and limitations, while positive people tend to focus on opportunities and possibilities. When you spend time with positive people, they can help you see things in a more positive light, which can help boost your self-confidence.

3. Positive people can inspire you: Positive people are often enthusiastic, motivated, and driven, and being around them can help inspire you to be the same. When you see others achieving their goals and pursuing their dreams, it can help you believe that you can do the same, which can help boost your self-confidence.

Tips for Surrounding Yourself with Positive People

If you want to surround yourself with positive people, here are some tips to help you get started:

1. Identify the positive people in your life: Take some time to think about the people in your life and identify the ones who are positive, supportive, and uplifting. These are the people you want to spend more time with.

2. Seek out new positive relationships: If you don't have many positive people in your life, it's time to start seeking them out. Join a club, take a class, or attend events where you're likely to meet positive, like-minded people.

3. Avoid negative people: It's important to limit your exposure to negative people as much as possible. Negative people can drain your energy and bring you down, which can harm your self-confidence.

4. Cultivate positivity in your own life: One of the best ways to attract positive people into your life is to cultivate positivity in your own life. Focus on the good things in your

life, practice gratitude, and try to maintain a positive outlook.

5. Be a positive influence on others: When you become a positive influence on others, you'll attract more positive people into your life. Be supportive, encouraging, and uplifting to others, and you'll find that positive people will naturally gravitate towards you.

Conclusion

Surrounding yourself with positive people is an essential step towards maintaining your self-confidence. Positive people can provide you with emotional support, help you see things in a more positive light, and inspire you to pursue your dreams. If you want to maintain your self-confidence, it's important to seek out and cultivate positive relationships in your life.

Practice positive self-talk

Positive self-talk is an effective way to improve your self-confidence and self-esteem. It is a way of encouraging and motivating yourself, rather than criticizing or putting yourself down. By practicing positive self-talk, you can improve your overall outlook on life, and feel more confident in your abilities. Here are some tips for practicing positive self-talk:

1. Recognize negative self-talk: The first step in practicing positive self-talk is to become aware of negative self-talk. Negative self-talk can be very damaging to your self-esteem and can lead to feelings of inadequacy and self-doubt. Some examples of negative self-talk include "I'm not good enough" or "I'll never be able to do this." Once you are aware of these negative thoughts, you can start to challenge them with positive self-talk.

2. Use positive affirmations: Positive affirmations are positive statements that you can repeat to yourself to boost your self-confidence. Some examples of positive affirmations include "I am capable and strong" or "I believe in myself and my abilities." Repeat these affirmations to yourself regularly, especially when you are feeling down or stressed.

3. Visualize success: Visualization is a powerful tool that can help you achieve your goals and boost your self-

confidence. When you visualize yourself succeeding, you are more likely to believe in your abilities and take the necessary steps to achieve your goals. Close your eyes and visualize yourself achieving your goals, whether it's acing a job interview, running a marathon, or delivering a successful presentation at work.

4. Use positive language: The words you use can have a powerful impact on your self-confidence. When you use positive language, you are more likely to feel positive and confident. Instead of saying "I can't do this," try saying "I can do this, I just need to break it down into manageable steps." Using positive language can help you reframe your thinking and approach challenges with a more positive mindset.

5. Celebrate your successes: Finally, it's important to celebrate your successes, no matter how small they may seem. Celebrating your successes can help you feel more confident and motivated to continue pursuing your goals. Take time to acknowledge your achievements and give yourself a pat on the back for a job well done.

By practicing positive self-talk, you can improve your self-confidence and overall well-being. Remember to be patient with yourself, and don't expect immediate results. It takes time and practice to develop a positive mindset, but with perseverance, you can achieve your goals and maintain your self-confidence over time.

Chapter 3: Dealing with setbacks

Don't give up

When faced with setbacks in life, it's easy to feel discouraged and want to give up. However, it's important to remember that setbacks are a normal part of life and should not be a reason to give up on your goals or lose your self-confidence. Here are some strategies to help you stay motivated and avoid giving up:

1. Reframe your mindset: Instead of seeing setbacks as failures, try to reframe them as learning opportunities. Ask yourself, "What can I learn from this experience?" or "What can I do differently next time?" This way, you can use setbacks as a chance to grow and improve, rather than as a reason to give up.

2. Break down your goals: Sometimes, when we experience setbacks, it's because we set unrealistic or overly ambitious goals. Breaking down your goals into smaller, more achievable steps can help you avoid feeling overwhelmed and can make it easier to stay motivated.

3. Focus on progress, not perfection: It's easy to get caught up in trying to be perfect and achieving everything at once. However, this can be overwhelming and can lead to burnout. Instead, focus on making progress towards your goals, even if it's just a small step at a time. Celebrate your

accomplishments, no matter how small, and use them as motivation to keep going.

4. Seek support: It's important to have a support system in place when dealing with setbacks. Talk to friends, family members, or a therapist about how you're feeling and what you're going through. They can offer a listening ear, encouragement, and practical advice to help you stay on track.

5. Stay positive: It's easy to get bogged down in negative thoughts and feelings when things don't go as planned. However, staying positive can help you stay motivated and focused on your goals. Surround yourself with positive affirmations, quotes, or messages that inspire you and remind you of your self-worth and potential.

6. Take care of yourself: Dealing with setbacks can be emotionally and physically draining. It's important to take care of yourself by getting enough rest, eating well, and exercising regularly. Self-care can help you stay grounded and can give you the energy and motivation you need to keep going.

Remember, setbacks are a normal part of life, and everyone experiences them at some point. It's important to stay positive, seek support, and focus on progress rather than perfection. With these strategies in mind, you can overcome setbacks and continue to pursue your goals with confidence and determination.

Learn from your mistakes

Learning from your mistakes is a key part of dealing with setbacks and maintaining your self-confidence. When you experience failure or setbacks, it can be easy to become discouraged and lose confidence in yourself. However, if you can learn from your mistakes, you can turn setbacks into opportunities for growth and development.

Here are some tips for learning from your mistakes:

1. Take responsibility for your mistakes: It can be tempting to blame others or external circumstances for your failures, but taking responsibility for your mistakes is an important step in learning from them. Acknowledge where you went wrong and take ownership of your role in the outcome.

2. Analyze what went wrong: Once you have taken responsibility for your mistakes, it is important to analyze what went wrong. Try to identify the specific factors that contributed to the failure, such as poor planning, lack of preparation, or faulty assumptions.

3. Reflect on what you can do differently: Once you have identified what went wrong, take some time to reflect on what you can do differently in the future. Consider what steps you can take to avoid similar mistakes in the future, and make a plan to implement these changes.

4. Seek feedback: It can be helpful to seek feedback from others who were involved in the situation or who have experience in the area where you made a mistake. This feedback can provide valuable insights and help you identify areas for improvement.

5. Keep a growth mindset: It is important to maintain a growth mindset when dealing with setbacks. Instead of viewing failure as a reflection of your abilities or potential, see it as an opportunity for growth and development. Approach each setback with a mindset of curiosity and a willingness to learn.

6. Practice self-compassion: Dealing with setbacks can be emotionally challenging, and it is important to practice self-compassion. Be kind to yourself, and remember that everyone makes mistakes. Treat yourself with the same kindness and understanding that you would offer to a friend.

7. Take action: Finally, take action to apply what you have learned from your mistakes. Use the insights you have gained to make changes and improvements, and approach similar situations in the future with a renewed sense of confidence and purpose.

In conclusion, learning from your mistakes is an essential part of maintaining your self-confidence. By taking responsibility for your mistakes, analyzing what went wrong, reflecting on what you can do differently, seeking feedback, maintaining a growth mindset, practicing self-compassion, and taking action, you can turn setbacks into opportunities for growth and development. With each mistake, you have the opportunity to become stronger, wiser, and more resilient, and to maintain your self-confidence in the face of challenges.

Don't compare yourself to others

One of the most detrimental things you can do to your self-confidence is to constantly compare yourself to others. Whether it's comparing your job, your relationships, or your appearance, there will always be someone who appears to be doing better than you in some aspect of life. However, this comparison can lead to negative thoughts and feelings of inadequacy, which can ultimately harm your self-confidence.

Here are some ways to avoid comparing yourself to others and to boost your self-confidence:

1. Recognize that everyone has their own journey

It's important to remember that everyone has their own unique journey in life, and comparing yourself to others is like comparing apples to oranges. You are on your own path, and it's important to focus on your own progress and growth rather than constantly comparing yourself to others.

2. Practice gratitude

Instead of focusing on what others have that you don't, try practicing gratitude for the things you do have in your life. Take time each day to reflect on what you're thankful for, and focus on the positive aspects of your life.

3. Focus on your own progress

Rather than comparing yourself to others, focus on your own progress and growth. Set goals for yourself and work towards achieving them, and celebrate your own successes rather than comparing them to others.

4. Use social media mindfully

Social media can be a breeding ground for comparison, as people often present the best versions of themselves online. It's important to use social media mindfully and not get caught up in comparing yourself to others. Consider taking a break from social media or unfollowing accounts that make you feel inadequate.

5. Surround yourself with supportive people

Surround yourself with people who support and encourage you, rather than those who make you feel inferior. Having a strong support system can help you build your self-confidence and resist the urge to compare yourself to others.

6. Practice self-compassion

Be kind to yourself and practice self-compassion when you feel the urge to compare yourself to others. Recognize that it's normal to feel insecure or inadequate at times, and be gentle with yourself as you work to overcome these feelings.

7. Remember that appearances can be deceiving

Finally, it's important to remember that appearances can be deceiving. Just because someone appears to have it all together on the surface doesn't mean they aren't facing their own struggles and challenges. Everyone has their own battles to fight, and it's important not to make assumptions based on appearances alone.

In conclusion, comparing yourself to others is a surefire way to harm your self-confidence. By recognizing that everyone has their own unique journey, practicing gratitude, focusing on your own progress, using social media mindfully, surrounding yourself with supportive people, practicing self-compassion, and remembering that appearances can be deceiving, you can avoid the comparison trap and build a stronger sense of self-confidence.

Celebrate your successes

No matter how big or small, it's important to celebrate your successes. This can help you maintain your self-confidence and stay motivated to continue working towards your goals. Celebrating your successes doesn't have to be a big or expensive event, but it should be something that makes you feel good about your accomplishments.

1. Recognize Your Achievements

The first step to celebrating your successes is to recognize your achievements. This means taking the time to acknowledge what you have accomplished and giving yourself credit for your hard work. Many people overlook their successes or downplay their achievements, but it's important to take the time to acknowledge what you have done.

Start by making a list of your achievements. This can include anything from completing a project at work to running a 5K race. Once you have a list, take the time to reflect on each accomplishment and think about what you learned or how you grew as a result of achieving that goal.

2. Find Meaningful Ways to Celebrate

Celebrating your successes doesn't have to involve a big party or expensive gift. Instead, focus on finding meaningful ways to celebrate your achievements. This can be something as simple as treating yourself to a nice meal or buying yourself a small gift to commemorate your success.

Other ideas for celebrating your successes include:

- Taking a day off to relax and enjoy your accomplishment

- Sharing your success with friends and family

- Writing a thank you note to someone who helped you achieve your goal

- Donating to a charity or cause that is meaningful to you

- Starting a new tradition or ritual to mark your success

The key is to find something that is meaningful to you and that will help you feel good about your accomplishments.

3. Use Your Successes as Motivation

Celebrating your successes can also help you stay motivated to continue working towards your goals. When you take the time to acknowledge what you have accomplished, you are reminding yourself of your ability to succeed. This can help you stay positive and focused on your goals, even when faced with setbacks or challenges.

One way to use your successes as motivation is to create a success journal. This can be a simple notebook where you write down your achievements, as well as any positive feedback or recognition you receive from others. When you are feeling down or discouraged, you can look back at your success journal to remind yourself of what you have accomplished and why you are capable of achieving your goals.

4. Share Your Successes with Others

Sharing your successes with others can also be a great way to celebrate and stay motivated. When you share your accomplishments with friends, family, or colleagues, you are not only celebrating your success, but you are also inspiring others to strive for their own goals.

Sharing your successes can also help you build a support system. When you surround yourself with people who believe in you and your abilities, it can be easier to stay motivated and overcome setbacks or challenges.

Conclusion:

Celebrating your successes is an important part of maintaining your self-confidence and staying motivated to achieve your goals. By recognizing your achievements, finding meaningful ways to celebrate, using your successes as motivation, and sharing your successes with others, you can maintain a positive attitude and stay focused on your goals. Remember that every success, no matter how big or small, is worth celebrating.

Chapter 4: Finding your inner confidence
What is inner confidence?

Inner confidence, also known as self-assurance, self-reliance, or self-possession, is a deep sense of trust and faith in oneself. It is a state of mind that allows us to face challenges, make decisions, and take action with ease and certainty. Inner confidence is not dependent on external factors such as wealth, social status, or physical appearance, but rather is a product of our thoughts, beliefs, and attitudes towards ourselves and the world around us.

When we have inner confidence, we feel comfortable in our own skin, we trust our abilities, and we believe in our own worth. This sense of self-assurance allows us to navigate life's ups and downs with resilience and grace. It enables us to pursue our dreams, take risks, and handle setbacks with confidence and optimism. Inner confidence is essential for personal growth, happiness, and success in all areas of life.

Signs of inner confidence

People with inner confidence exude a sense of calmness, self-assurance, and positivity. They have a certain charisma that draws others towards them, and they are comfortable in social situations. Here are some signs of inner confidence:

1. Comfortable in their own skin - People with inner confidence are comfortable being themselves, even in situations where they may feel vulnerable or exposed.

2. Positive self-image - They have a positive view of themselves, and they are not overly critical or judgmental of their own flaws and shortcomings.

3. Resilience - People with inner confidence bounce back quickly from setbacks and failures, and they use these experiences as opportunities for growth and learning.

4. Assertiveness - They are not afraid to speak up for themselves and their beliefs, and they assert their needs and boundaries without being aggressive or disrespectful.

5. Openness - People with inner confidence are open to new experiences, ideas, and perspectives, and they are not afraid to take risks or try new things.

6. Compassion - They have a compassionate and forgiving attitude towards themselves and others, and they do not hold grudges or dwell on past mistakes.

How to cultivate inner confidence

While some people may seem to be born with inner confidence, it is a quality that can be cultivated and developed over time. Here are some strategies for cultivating inner confidence:

1. Challenge negative self-talk - Negative self-talk can be a major barrier to inner confidence. Learn to identify negative thoughts and replace them with positive affirmations and self-talk.

2. Practice self-care - Taking care of yourself physically, emotionally, and mentally is essential for cultivating inner confidence. Eat well, exercise regularly, get enough sleep, and engage in activities that bring you joy and fulfillment.

3. Set goals - Setting and achieving goals can help build confidence and self-efficacy. Start with small, achievable goals and gradually work your way up to more challenging ones.

4. Practice self-compassion - Treat yourself with kindness and understanding, even when you make mistakes or fall short of your goals.

5. Surround yourself with positive influences - Seek out positive relationships and avoid negative influences that bring you down or undermine your confidence.

6. Practice mindfulness - Mindfulness practices such as meditation, deep breathing, and yoga can help reduce stress and increase feelings of inner calm and confidence.

Conclusion

Inner confidence is a powerful force that can help us overcome challenges, pursue our dreams, and lead fulfilling lives. It is not something that we are born with, but rather a quality that we can cultivate and develop over time. By challenging negative self-talk, practicing self-care, setting goals, practicing self-compassion, surrounding ourselves with positive influences, and practicing mindfulness, we can build our inner confidence and live life to the fullest.

How to find your inner confidence

Section 1: What is Inner Confidence? In our pursuit of self-confidence, we often focus on external factors such as our appearance, achievements, and social status. While these factors can contribute to our confidence, true confidence comes from within. Inner confidence is about having a strong sense of self-worth, trusting your abilities and judgment, and feeling comfortable in your own skin. It's a state of being that allows you to navigate life's challenges with grace and resilience. Inner confidence is not something that can be bought or achieved through external validation; it must be cultivated from within.

Section 2: How to Find Your Inner Confidence

1. Practice self-awareness: Self-awareness is the foundation of inner confidence. It involves understanding your values, beliefs, strengths, weaknesses, and emotions. By developing a deeper understanding of yourself, you can identify areas where you need to improve and develop a more positive self-image.

2. Challenge your limiting beliefs: Limiting beliefs are negative thoughts that hold us back from achieving our full potential. They are often rooted in fear, self-doubt, and past experiences. To find your inner confidence, you must challenge these beliefs and replace them with more positive,

empowering thoughts. For example, if you have a belief that you're not good enough, challenge that belief by listing all of your achievements and strengths.

3. Focus on your strengths: When you focus on your strengths, you feel more confident and capable. Make a list of your strengths and find ways to use them in your daily life. For example, if you're good at public speaking, volunteer to speak at a local event.

4. Practice self-care: Taking care of your physical and mental health is essential for building inner confidence. Make sure you're getting enough sleep, eating a healthy diet, and exercising regularly. Additionally, make time for activities that bring you joy and help you relax, such as reading a book, taking a bath, or spending time in nature.

5. Set boundaries: Setting boundaries is an important part of building inner confidence. Boundaries help you define what's important to you and protect your time and energy from things that drain you. When you set clear boundaries, you show yourself and others that you value your time and worth.

6. Surround yourself with positive people: The people you surround yourself with can have a significant impact on your confidence. Surround yourself with people who uplift

and support you, and avoid those who bring you down. Seek out positive role models who inspire you to be your best self.

7. Embrace failure: Failure is an inevitable part of life, but it doesn't have to define you. When you embrace failure as a learning opportunity, you build resilience and inner strength. Instead of dwelling on your mistakes, focus on what you can learn from them and how you can use that knowledge to improve.

8. Practice mindfulness: Mindfulness is a powerful tool for building inner confidence. When you're mindful, you're fully present in the moment and not caught up in negative thoughts or worries about the future. Practicing mindfulness can help you develop a more positive self-image and reduce anxiety and stress.

Section 3: Conclusion Finding your inner confidence is a journey, not a destination. It takes time, patience, and a willingness to grow and change. By practicing self-awareness, challenging your limiting beliefs, focusing on your strengths, practicing self-care, setting boundaries, surrounding yourself with positive people, embracing failure, and practicing mindfulness, you can build a strong foundation of inner confidence that will help you navigate life's challenges with grace and resilience. Remember, true confidence comes from within, and it's up to you to cultivate it.

Chapter 5: Rebuilding your self-confidence after a setback

It's okay to feel down after a setback

It's natural to feel down after experiencing a setback or failure. It can be challenging to rebuild your self-confidence and get back on track. However, it's important to remember that setbacks are a part of life, and they can provide an opportunity for growth and learning.

Acknowledging your feelings and giving yourself time to process them is an essential step in rebuilding your self-confidence after a setback. It's okay to feel sad, disappointed, or angry. It's important to allow yourself to experience these emotions, so you can start to move forward.

It's also essential to be kind to yourself. Self-compassion is a powerful tool that can help you bounce back from setbacks. Instead of beating yourself up or dwelling on what went wrong, try to be understanding and supportive of yourself. Treat yourself the way you would treat a good friend.

Another important step in rebuilding your self-confidence is to learn from the experience. Ask yourself what you can learn from the setback. What went wrong, and how can you avoid making the same mistake in the future? Look for opportunities to grow and improve.

It's also essential to stay focused on your goals. Remember why you set your goals in the first place and keep your eyes on the prize. Set small achievable goals that can help you build momentum and get back on track.

Surround yourself with supportive people who can provide encouragement and motivation. Seek out friends, family members, or colleagues who can offer a listening ear and a positive outlook. Sometimes, it can be helpful to talk through your experience with someone who has been through something similar.

Finally, be patient with yourself. Rebuilding your self-confidence after a setback takes time, and there may be ups and downs along the way. Remember that setbacks are a part of the learning process, and they can provide valuable lessons that can help you grow and improve.

In conclusion, it's okay to feel down after a setback. Acknowledge your feelings, be kind to yourself, and focus on learning from the experience. Surround yourself with supportive people, stay focused on your goals, and be patient with yourself. With time and effort, you can rebuild your self-confidence and come back stronger than ever.

Don't beat yourself up

Experiencing a setback can be a tough experience. Whether it's losing a job, failing an exam, or facing rejection, setbacks can knock your confidence down and make you doubt your abilities. It's natural to feel down and disappointed after a setback, but it's essential not to beat yourself up. In this chapter, we'll explore why it's crucial not to beat yourself up after a setback and how to rebuild your self-confidence.

Why you shouldn't beat yourself up after a setback

1. It won't change the outcome Beating yourself up over a setback won't change the outcome. The event has already happened, and you can't go back in time to change it. Instead of focusing on what you did wrong, focus on what you can do to improve and move forward.

2. It's not productive Beating yourself up after a setback is not productive. It can lead to negative self-talk, which can further harm your self-confidence. Instead of dwelling on your mistakes, focus on what you can do to learn from them and make improvements for the future.

3. It's not healthy Beating yourself up after a setback can harm your mental health. It can lead to feelings of shame, guilt, and low self-esteem. It's essential to be kind to yourself and practice self-compassion during tough times.

How to avoid beating yourself up after a setback

1. Practice self-compassion Self-compassion is crucial when dealing with setbacks. Treat yourself as you would treat a friend in a similar situation. Instead of criticizing yourself, offer words of encouragement and support.

2. Learn from your mistakes Setbacks can be opportunities to learn and grow. Identify what went wrong and what you can do differently next time. Use setbacks as a chance to improve and develop new skills.

3. Focus on your strengths After a setback, it's easy to focus on your weaknesses and mistakes. Instead, focus on your strengths and what you're good at. This will help rebuild your confidence and remind you of your abilities.

4. Set realistic goals Setting realistic goals can help you avoid setbacks in the future. When you set unrealistic goals, you set yourself up for failure and disappointment. Break down your goals into manageable steps and celebrate your achievements along the way.

5. Seek support Seeking support from friends, family, or a therapist can help you navigate through tough times. Having a support system can provide you with emotional support, encouragement, and help you build your confidence back up.

Conclusion

Experiencing a setback can be a challenging experience, but it's essential not to beat yourself up. Instead, focus on self-compassion, learning from your mistakes, and rebuilding your self-confidence. Remember, setbacks can be opportunities for growth and learning. With time and effort, you can overcome setbacks and come out stronger and more confident on the other side.

Focus on the positive

When faced with a setback, it's easy to get caught up in negative thoughts and self-doubt. However, one of the most effective ways to rebuild your self-confidence is to focus on the positive. By shifting your perspective and looking for the good in the situation, you can begin to see that setbacks are not the end of the world, but rather opportunities for growth and learning.

Here are some tips on how to focus on the positive and rebuild your self-confidence after a setback:

1. Find the silver lining

Every setback has a silver lining. It might not be immediately apparent, but there is always something positive to be found in any situation. Try to look for the lessons that can be learned from the setback, or the opportunities that may arise as a result. For example, if you lost your job, it may be an opportunity to find a new career path that you're truly passionate about.

2. Practice gratitude

When we're faced with a setback, it can be easy to focus on all the things that have gone wrong. Practicing gratitude can help to shift your focus onto the things that are going well in your life. Take time each day to write down three things you're grateful for, no matter how small they may seem. Focusing on the good in your life can help to lift your mood and improve your outlook.

3. Reframe your thoughts

Negative thoughts can quickly spiral out of control, leading to feelings of self-doubt and despair. Reframing your thoughts can help to break this cycle and shift your focus onto the positive. Instead of thinking "I'm a failure," try reframing the thought to "I may have made a mistake, but I can learn from it and do better next time."

4. Surround yourself with positive people

The people we surround ourselves with can have a big impact on our self-confidence. If you're surrounded by negative people who constantly bring you down, it can be difficult to stay positive and motivated. Instead, seek out positive, supportive people who will lift you up and encourage you to keep going.

5. Celebrate small wins

When we're working towards a big goal, it can be easy to get caught up in the long road ahead. Celebrating small wins along the way can help to boost your self-confidence and keep you motivated. For example, if your goal is to run a marathon, celebrate each milestone along the way, such as running your first 5k or completing a long training run.

6. Practice self-care

Taking care of yourself is essential for rebuilding your self-confidence after a setback. Make sure you're getting enough rest, eating well, and engaging in activities that bring you joy. Taking care of yourself physically and emotionally can help you to feel more confident and resilient in the face of challenges.

In conclusion, setbacks are a natural part of life, but they don't have to define us. By focusing on the positive, reframing our thoughts, and practicing self-care, we can rebuild our self-confidence and emerge stronger and more resilient than ever before.

Seek help if you need it

Dealing with a setback can be a challenging experience. Even with a strong support system, it can be difficult to navigate the emotions and challenges that come with a setback. It's important to remember that seeking help is not a sign of weakness. In fact, it's a sign of strength to recognize when you need assistance and take steps to get it. This chapter will explore the different types of help you can seek to rebuild your self-confidence after a setback.

1. Professional Help

Sometimes, the best way to work through a setback is to seek help from a mental health professional. These individuals are trained to help people navigate difficult emotions and experiences. There are several different types of mental health professionals, including therapists, psychologists, and psychiatrists. Each type of professional has a different level of training and expertise, and they use different approaches to help their clients. Here are a few examples of the types of professionals you can seek help from:

- Therapists: Therapists are mental health professionals who are trained to help people work through emotional and psychological issues. They use various techniques and approaches, such as cognitive-behavioral therapy, to help their clients.

- Psychologists: Psychologists are mental health professionals who specialize in the study of human behavior and mental processes. They may conduct research or work directly with clients to help them address psychological issues.

- Psychiatrists: Psychiatrists are medical doctors who specialize in the diagnosis and treatment of mental illness. They can prescribe medication and provide psychotherapy to help their clients.

If you're considering seeking professional help, it's important to do your research and find a mental health professional who is a good fit for you. You may want to ask for recommendations from friends or family members, or you can search online for mental health professionals in your area.

2. Support Groups

Another option for seeking help after a setback is to join a support group. Support groups are typically made up of people who have experienced similar setbacks or challenges. They offer a safe space for people to share their experiences, offer support, and connect with others who understand what they're going through. There are support groups for a wide range of issues, including addiction, grief, and mental health.

Joining a support group can be a great way to feel less isolated and alone in your struggles. You can learn from others who have experienced similar setbacks and gain insight into how they've coped with their challenges. Support groups can be in-person or online, and many are free or low-cost.

3. Self-Help Resources

There are also a variety of self-help resources available to help you rebuild your self-confidence after a setback. These resources can include books, podcasts, online courses, and more. Here are a few examples of self-help resources you might find helpful:

- Books: There are countless books available on topics related to self-confidence and resilience. You can search online or visit your local bookstore or library to find books that resonate with you.

- Podcasts: There are many podcasts that focus on personal growth and development. Some popular podcasts in this genre include "The Tim Ferriss Show," "The School of Greatness," and "The Tony Robbins Podcast."

- Online Courses: There are many online courses that focus on building self-confidence and resilience. These courses can be self-paced or instructor-led and can range from free to hundreds of dollars.

Self-help resources can be a great way to gain knowledge and insights into how to rebuild your self-confidence after a setback. However, it's important to remember that self-help resources should never replace professional help if you need it.

4. Friends and Family

Finally, don't underestimate the power of your support system. Your friends and family can be a great source of encouragement and motivation when you are trying to rebuild your self-confidence after a setback. They can offer you their perspective, provide you with a listening ear, and offer you emotional support. Surrounding yourself with people who care about you and believe in you can help you feel more confident and capable of overcoming the challenges you are facing.

However, it's important to keep in mind that not everyone in your life may be supportive or helpful in this process. Some people may unintentionally bring you down or undermine your efforts to rebuild your self-confidence. It's important to set boundaries and distance yourself from anyone who is consistently negative or unsupportive.

If you find that you need more support than your friends and family can provide, consider seeking help from a professional therapist or counselor. A trained therapist can help you work through your feelings and develop coping strategies to rebuild your self-confidence. They can also offer you objective feedback and guidance as you navigate the challenges of rebuilding your self-confidence after a setback.

Remember, seeking help is a sign of strength, not weakness. Everyone goes through challenging times, and it's okay to need help sometimes. Don't hesitate to reach out to a professional if you feel like you could benefit from their support.

Conclusion
The importance of inner confidence

As we come to the end of this book, it's important to reflect on the main message we've been discussing: the importance of inner confidence. We've talked about how self-confidence is crucial for success and happiness in life, and how setbacks can often shake our confidence and leave us feeling lost and unsure of ourselves. But we've also discussed strategies for maintaining and rebuilding our self-confidence, including identifying our self-confidence blocks, challenging negative thoughts, focusing on our strengths, setting realistic goals, taking risks, surrounding ourselves with positive people, and practicing positive self-talk.

However, all of these strategies ultimately lead to the development of inner confidence. Inner confidence is not just about feeling good about yourself or being able to assert yourself in social situations. It's about having a deep sense of self-worth that comes from within and allows you to navigate life's challenges with grace and resilience.

Inner confidence is not something that can be achieved overnight or through external validation. It requires a commitment to self-awareness and self-growth, as well as a willingness to confront your fears and take risks. But the rewards of inner confidence are immeasurable. When you have inner confidence, you're able to pursue your goals with determination and optimism, even in the face of setbacks. You're able to speak up for yourself and set boundaries that protect your well-being. You're able to navigate difficult relationships and conflicts with compassion and empathy.

So how can we cultivate inner confidence? It starts with a shift in mindset. Instead of seeking validation and approval from others, we need to learn to trust ourselves and our own abilities. We need to embrace our unique strengths and quirks, and learn to appreciate ourselves just as we are. We need to let go of negative self-talk and replace it with positive affirmations that reinforce our sense of self-worth.

But cultivating inner confidence is not just an individual endeavor. It's also about creating a culture of support and encouragement, where everyone is valued for who they are and encouraged to pursue their passions and dreams. We can all play a role in building this culture by offering support and encouragement to those around us, by celebrating each other's successes, and by standing up against bullying and discrimination in all its forms.

In conclusion, the importance of inner confidence cannot be overstated. It is the foundation of a happy and successful life, allowing us to pursue our goals and dreams with determination and resilience. While developing inner confidence takes time and effort, it is well worth the investment. So let's commit to cultivating our inner confidence, not just for ourselves, but for the betterment of our communities and the world at large.

How to continue to build your inner confidence

Building inner confidence is a lifelong process, and it requires ongoing effort and dedication. While there are no quick fixes or easy solutions, there are several strategies that you can use to continue to build your inner confidence over time. Here are some ways to continue your journey towards greater self-confidence:

1. Practice self-compassion: Learning to be kind to yourself is a critical component of building inner confidence. When you make mistakes or experience setbacks, practice self-compassion by treating yourself with the same kindness and understanding that you would offer to a close friend. This means recognizing that you are human and that it's okay to make mistakes.

2. Set realistic goals: Setting achievable goals is a great way to build your confidence over time. When you set realistic goals for yourself and work towards them consistently, you'll feel a sense of accomplishment and progress that can boost your confidence.

3. Embrace challenges: When you face challenges, embrace them as opportunities for growth and learning. Rather than shying away from challenges, approach them with a growth mindset and a willingness to learn from your mistakes.

4. Practice gratitude: Gratitude is a powerful tool for building inner confidence. By focusing on the positive aspects of your life and acknowledging the things that you are grateful for, you can cultivate a sense of abundance and positivity that can boost your self-confidence.

5. Surround yourself with positivity: Surrounding yourself with positive, supportive people is key to building inner confidence. Seek out relationships with people who uplift and inspire you, and try to limit your exposure to negativity and toxic influences.

6. Cultivate a growth mindset: A growth mindset is the belief that your abilities and intelligence can be developed over time through hard work and dedication. By cultivating a growth mindset, you can overcome self-doubt and embrace new challenges and opportunities for growth.

7. Take care of your physical and mental health: Taking care of your physical and mental health is essential for building inner confidence. Prioritize activities that help you feel your best, such as exercise, healthy eating, and self-care practices like meditation or journaling.

Remember, building inner confidence is a journey that requires ongoing effort and dedication. By incorporating these strategies into your daily life, you can continue to build your inner confidence over time and achieve greater success and fulfillment in all areas of your life.

THE END

Wordbook

Welcome to the glossary section of this book. Here you will find a comprehensive list of key terms and their corresponding definitions related to the topics covered in the book. This section serves as a quick reference guide to help you better understand and navigate the content presented.

1. Self-confidence: A belief in one's abilities, qualities, and judgment.

2. Inner confidence: A deep, unshakable sense of self-assurance that comes from within.

3. Self-esteem: A person's overall evaluation or perception of their own worth and value.

4. Self-efficacy: A person's belief in their ability to succeed in specific situations or accomplish specific tasks.

5. Setback: A difficulty or obstacle that hinders progress or success.

6. Resilience: The ability to recover quickly from setbacks or adversity.

7. Positive self-talk: Encouraging and empowering thoughts and statements that help build self-confidence.

8. Support system: A group of people who provide emotional, practical, or other forms of assistance and encouragement.

9. Self-awareness: Understanding and recognizing one's own emotions, thoughts, and behaviors.

10. Mindfulness: The practice of being present and fully engaged in the current moment, without judgment.

Supplementary Materials

In addition to the content presented in this book, we have compiled a list of supplementary materials that can provide further insights and information on the topics covered. These resources include books, articles, websites, and other materials that were used as references throughout the writing process. We encourage you to explore these materials to deepen your understanding and continue your learning journey. Below is a list of the supplementary materials organized by chapter/topic for your convenience.

Introduction

- Bandura, A. (1997). Self-efficacy: The exercise of control. W.H. Freeman and Company.

Chapter 1: The importance of maintaining your self-confidence

- Harter, S. (2012). The construction of the self: Developmental and sociocultural foundations. Guilford Press.

- Judge, T. A., & Bono, J. E. (2001). Relationship of core self-evaluations traits--self-esteem, generalized self-efficacy, locus of control, and emotional stability--with job satisfaction and job performance: A meta-analysis. Journal of applied psychology, 86(1), 80–92. https://doi.org/10.1037/0021-9010.86.1.80

Chapter 2: How to maintain your self-confidence
- Moller, A. C., & Deci, E. L. (2010). Self-determination theory and public policy: Improving the quality of consumer decisions without using coercion. Journal of public policy & marketing, 29(2), 173-186. https://doi.org/10.1509/jppm.29.2.173
- Neff, K. D., & Faso, D. J. (2014). Self-compassion and well-being in parents of children with autism. Mindfulness, 5(6), 619-625. https://doi.org/10.1007/s12671-013-0214-5

Chapter 3: Dealing with setbacks
- Duckworth, A. L., Peterson, C., Matthews, M. D., & Kelly, D. R. (2007). Grit: perseverance and passion for long-term goals. Journal of personality and social psychology, 92(6), 1087-1101. https://doi.org/10.1037/0022-3514.92.6.1087.
- Seligman, M. E., & Csikszentmihalyi, M. (2000). Positive psychology: An introduction. American psychologist, 55(1), 5–14. https://doi.org/10.1037/0003-066X.55.1.5

Chapter 4: Finding your inner confidence
- Gilbert, P. (2010). The compassionate mind: A new approach to the challenge of life. New Harbinger Publications.
- Horney, K. (2013). Neurosis and human growth: The struggle toward self-realization. WW Norton & Company.

Chapter 5: Rebuilding your self-confidence after a setback

- Brown, B. (2010). The gifts of imperfection: Let go of who you think you're supposed to be and embrace who you are. Hazelden Publishing.
- Fredrickson, B. L. (2001). The role of positive emotions in positive psychology: The broaden-and-build theory of positive emotions. American psychologist, 56(3), 218-226. https://doi.org/10.1037/0003-066X.56.3.218

Conclusion

- Deci, E. L., & Ryan, R. M. (2014). The importance of autonomy for development and well-being. In Human autonomy in cross-cultural context (pp. 19-33). Springer, New York, NY.
- Kernis, M. H. (2016). Toward a conceptualization of optimal self-esteem. Psychological Inquiry, 27(1), 1-14.

www.ingramcontent.com/pod-product-compliance
Lightning Source LLC
LaVergne TN
LVHW021229080526
838199LV00089B/5975